Salut!

Teacher Handbook

This brilliant little book is an indispensable guide to getting the most out of CGP *Salut!* in your French lessons for Years 3-6.

The first section introduces all the interactive features and printable resources, with plenty of ideas for extra activities and extension work.

After that, there's a **Basic Grammar Guide** that explains all the technical rules you'll need to teach French effectively at Key Stage 2!

Section One — Teaching with Salut!

The first half of this **Teacher Handbook** introduces all the different features of *Salut!*, and is packed with **tips** to help you get the most out of your resources.

Section Two — Basic Grammar Guide

This section explains some of the more **technical aspects** of the language, to help you feel **confident** and **secure** in your French teaching.

An Introduction to Salut!

Welcome to CGP *Salut!*

Salut! is a **full set** of teaching resources based around the **interactive whiteboard** (IWB). All our resources are presented in a fun and friendly way, to help you **deliver** engaging **French lessons** to all your KS2 pupils.

We've got the Programme of Study covered

Salut! is **more** than just an interactive whiteboard resource. It includes a full **Scheme of Work**, complete with **lesson outlines** and practical **classroom activities** to support your teaching.

The Scheme of Work is **fully mapped** to the KS2 Programme of Study for foreign languages — with each PoS statement broken down into measurable **Learning Outcomes** for each year.

Packed with games, songs and stories to engage your class

Every lesson has a range of fun, interactive **games** to help your pupils build **listening** and **reading** skills.

And for each unit, there's a simple, catchy **song** in **karaoke format** and a fully illustrated **story** to help your pupils to **engage** with the language.

Don't worry if your French is a bit shaky

Salut! has been designed to be used by **any** teacher, whether you know **some** French, **lots** of it or **none** at all. There are **audio recordings** of all the **French** content and everything has an **English translation**, so you **don't** need any **prior knowledge** of the language.

Please see the Quick Start Guide for help with installing the program.

The Scheme of Work

The **individual resources** of *Salut!* can all be used **flexibly** to fit in with your school's existing curriculum.

But if you're **new** to French teaching, or are just looking for a **fresh** Scheme of Work, we've created a **clear, unit-based scheme** for you to follow.

The Scheme of Work is split into four Stages

The *Salut!* range contains **two separate discs**, which can be used together to cover the whole of KS2.

The Years 3-4 disc contains stages 1 & 2 of the Scheme of Work, and the Years 5-6 disc contains stages 3 & 4.

Stage 1 (Year 3)

Core Units 1 - 3, Animals, Food, At School

The first stage is aimed at **absolute beginners**. The Core Units introduce basic language like colours and numbers that will be **essential** for the rest of the course. It also has three **simple**, topic-based units to spark children's interest.

Stage 2 (Year 4)

Playtime, My Home, My Town, Describing People, The Body, Sport

Stage 2 starts to introduce some more **varied** language and sentence structures, including sentences in the **third person**. But all in contexts that the children will be **familiar with**.

Stage 3 (Year 5)

On Holiday, Eating Out, Hobbies, A School Trip, Seasons, The Environment

Stage 3 contains more **complex** vocabulary and sentence structures. Children will learn to use **adjectives** to add detail to their sentences, and talk about their hobbies and holidays.

Stage 4 (Year 6)

Actions, In France, Family, A Weekend with Friends, The Future, Jobs

Stage 4 gives children a **taste** of other tenses. Using the **perfect** and **near future** tenses, children will talk about what they've seen and done, and what they're going to do in the future.

The Years 5-6 disc also contains the **Core Units** from the Years 3-4 disc, so you can recap the basics with your class.

The Scheme of Work

Salut! is packed with resources, so here's a quick run-down of what's in a unit.

Teaching a Unit

- Each unit is designed to be taught over a **half-term**.
- There are **six lessons** in each unit.
- For each unit, you get:
    1. A detailed **Scheme of Work** document to help you plan engaging lessons for your class (see pages 26-28).

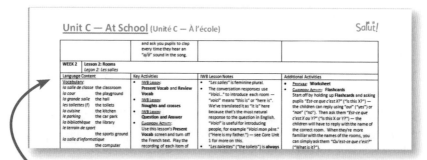

In here, you'll find suggested **activities** for each lesson — both IWB activities from the disc and practical classroom ideas. There are also **notes** on any tricky grammar or usage points that might crop up, and **links** to the **KS2 Programme of Study**.

    2. Five full **interactive lessons**, containing **teaching** activities and **games**. Near the start of each unit, there will be a **song lesson** (see p.14) to help engage your class with the theme of the unit.
    3. A **story lesson** at the end of the unit to tie it all together (see p.15).
    4. A set of **printable lesson resources** for every lesson (see pages 16-22) including worksheets, word lists and flashcards.

- The activities we suggest for a **lesson** don't necessarily have to be done in one hour-long session. Especially **early on**, it can be good to spread out your week's French teaching into a number of **shorter slots**. This gives your class chance to digest what they've learnt, and means they're less likely to feel **overwhelmed**.

The Main Menu

If you load *Salut!* and click on one of the **unit titles** down the left hand side, you'll see a screen like this one (this one's from the Years 3-4 disc).

Choose a unit

The **units** are listed down the left hand side of the screen. Click on one to see a list of the **six lessons** in the unit.

Search

If you're looking for a **particular** bit of vocab but don't know where to find it, try **searching** for it here. You can type in French or English.

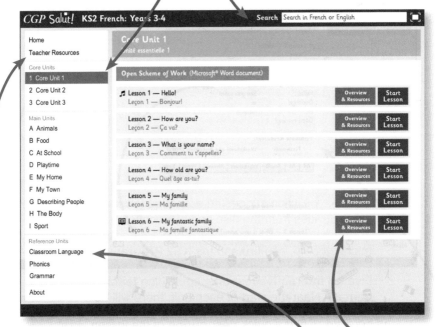

Teacher Resources

Here you'll find your **planning** and **tracking** documents (including the full Scheme of Work) (see pages 26-28), all **printable lesson resources** by unit (see pages 16-22) and a searchable copy of this book in Adobe® PDF format.

Overview & Resources

Click on one of these blue boxes to see **lesson details**.

Reference Units

Reference Units to help with **Classroom Language**, **Phonics** and **Grammar** can be found here. See pages 29-31 for more.

The Main Menu

Clicking '**Overview & Resources**' from the main menu opens up some extra details about the lesson, and shows you all the **printable resources** for it.

Scheme of Work

Open the **Scheme of Work** document for this unit here (see p.26).

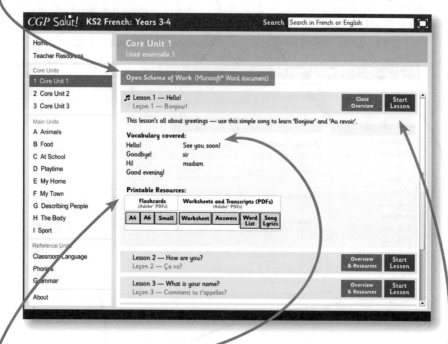

Lesson Overview

In here, you'll find a quick **description** of the lesson, a list (in English) of all the **vocabulary** covered and the sentence structures used in the '**Question and Answer**' section (see p.12).

Printable Resources

From here you can open and print all the printable resources for this lesson (see p.16): **worksheets**, **flashcards**, **word lists**, and **transcripts/ translations** of the song and story.

Start Lesson

Click on this red button to get to all your **interactive resources** for the lesson (see next page).

Starting your Lesson

When you **start** a lesson, you'll see a screen a bit like the one below.

Each lesson has two parts (or three if there's a song)

In the **top half** of the screen, you'll find **word-level** teaching activities (see p.8) and games (see p.10).

Click the **lesson title** to hear it spoken **aloud**.

Further down the screen, you'll find **sentence-level** activities (see p.12-13), to help the children put their new vocabulary into a **conversational context**.

Song lessons

If there's a **song** in the lesson, you'll find that in its own section at the bottom of the lesson menu.

Classroom Tips

All the lessons are laid out in the **same way** so you can easily find what you're looking for. But of course, you don't have to structure your **lesson** that way.

You might want to start with the **question** to put the French in **context**, do **all** the teaching before you play any games, or kick off your lesson with a **song**.

Teaching New Words

Each lesson includes two different screens for **teaching** the key vocabulary — 'Present Vocab' and '**Review Vocab**'.

The lesson's vocabulary is listed on the Lesson Overview (see p.6), and the Scheme of Work (see p.26), so you can familiarise yourself with it before the lesson.

Get to grips with the vocabulary using Present Vocab

This screen displays each item of vocabulary **individually** on its own page.

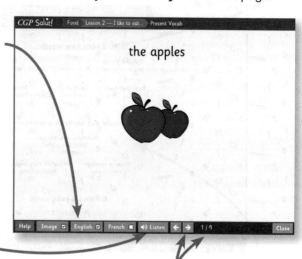

Choose what's visible

Click the tick boxes to **choose** what you want to display. You can choose to show the **image**, the **French text** and/or the **English text**.

Listen in French

Click '**Listen**' to hear the phrase spoken by a **native French speaker**.

Go through each word in turn

Use the **arrow buttons** to move between the different words in the lesson. The **counter** to the right of the arrows shows you how far through the list you are.

Classroom Tips

- **Before** you turn on the French **text**, play the **audio** a few times and ask the children to say the word back to you. *(If the French text is visible, some children will try to read it like English rather than picking up the correct pronunciation from the audio.)*

- Once pupils are familiar with the vocabulary, try **hiding** the image and the English text and asking pupils to tell you what the French word means. You could try this exercise using the French **text**, or by playing them the **audio**.

Teaching New Words

Review Vocab has all your vocabulary on one screen

The '**Review Vocab**' screen lets you work with **all** the words for the lesson at once.

This screen works a bit like a set of **flashcards**. The default setting is '**flip mode**' — when you click a card, it flips over to show the written French on the other side. Click it again to flip it back.

The **audio** also plays each time you click a card.

To flip, or not to flip...

You can turn off '**flip mode**' down here — now the cards don't turn over when you click, you just hear the **audio**.

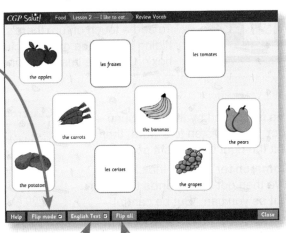

You can **turn off** the English text here.

Flip all

This button turns all the cards so they're the **same way up** — either all picture or all French text.

Classroom Tips

- This screen can be a useful backdrop for the **start** of your lesson.

- You could also use it **after** 'Present Vocab', or at the end of the lesson, as a **summary** activity. Here are a few ideas to try:

  1. Set all the cards **French-up**. Ask a volunteer to come up to the whiteboard and touch the card that says, e.g. "the strawberries".

  2. Again, set the cards **French-up**. Ask a volunteer to read one of the cards **aloud**. You can then play the **audio** to check their pronunciation.

  3. For a more advanced activity, start with the cards **picture-up**. Then ask for a volunteer to **recite** one of the French words from **memory**.

Playing Some Games

Each lesson in *Salut!* has a selection of **games** that draw on **listening**, **reading** and **memory** skills. In the top half of the **lesson menu** (see p.7), you'll find simple **word-level** games for your class to test their new vocabulary.

Listening Games

Beat that bee!

In this simple game, you just press the '**Écouter**' button to hear a word spoken aloud, then touch the **matching image** on screen.

To add a touch of fun, there's a bee with a box hiding behind the grid of pictures. What's in the box? Clear the images to find out.

Hit it!

This game is inspired by the fairground duck shoot. Pupils listen to a word, then have to hit the right image as it pops up.

Press '**Commencer**' to start the clock, and you've then got **30 seconds** to get as many right as you can. But be careful — hit the **wrong** image and you **lose** a point.

Classroom Tips

Try playing *Hit it!* as a **team** game. Have a team of three or four come to the board and **take turns** listening to a word and trying to hit the right image.

The team gets a **score** at the end of the game, which another team can try to beat.

Trolley Dash

On the left hand side of the screen is an audio '**shopping list**'.

Click the first '**Écouter**' button to hear an item from the list, this will start the timer.

Use the **trolley controls** to move around the screen and collect the item. Once you've got it, you'll be able to listen to the next one in the list, but you'll have to be quick — you've got just **three and a half minutes** to pick up all the items and get to the checkout.

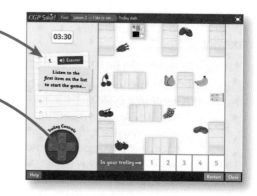

Playing Some Games

Word Games

Spell it!

In this game, you need to **unscramble a set of letters** to complete a French word or phrase, based on a picture clue. Once you think you've got it right, press '**Vérifier**' to check your answer — you've got three chances.

Hangman

This classic game **only appears on Disc 2**. Try to guess a word or phrase from the lesson by suggesting letters that might be in it.

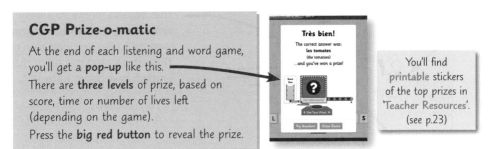

CGP Prize-o-matic

At the end of each listening and word game, you'll get a **pop-up** like this.
There are **three levels** of prize, based on score, time or number of lives left (depending on the game).
Press the **big red button** to reveal the prize.

Très bien!
The correct answer was:
les tomates
(the tomatoes)
...and you've won a prize!

You'll find printable stickers of the top prizes in 'Teacher Resources'. (see p.23)

2-Player Reading Games

Noughts and crosses

Choose a **French word** from a list and then select its matching picture in the grid to place a nought or cross.

Classroom Tips

These reading games are all for two players. Try splitting your class into **two teams** to play them, with representatives of each team coming up to play at the whiteboard.

Snap

One set of cards has **French words** and the other shows the **matching images**. To win a point, hit '**Bataille!**' when the image and word match. But be careful — if you're wrong you lose a point! The first to **three points** is the winner.

Pick-a-pair

This game **only appears on Disc 2**. Players take turns to select a **pair of cards** to reveal what's on them. If the cards show a French word and the **matching** image, they win a point and get another turn.

Putting New Words in Context

Speaking and writing in **sentences** is a key part of the Programme of Study. So in each lesson, there's a '**Question & Answer**' screen where the new vocabulary is put in a **conversational context**. (Most lessons on the Years 5-6 disc have two Question & Answer screens, but they work in the same way.)

Listen to the question

Click the image card on the left to **hear the question** and see the French text.

In some lessons, there'll be more than one question to choose from.

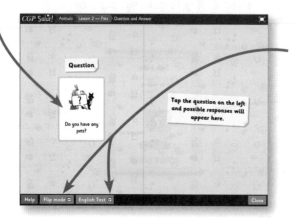

This screen works in a very similar way to '**Review Vocab**' (see p.9). So you can turn off '**flip mode**' and get rid of the English text down here.

Pupils will need to have learnt the lesson's vocabulary (see p.8-9) to respond.

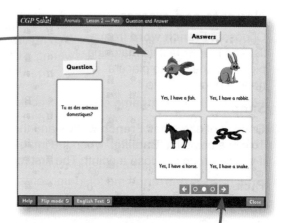

Choose an answer

Click on any of the answer cards that appear on the right — you'll hear the French audio, and the card will '**flip**' to show the French text.

Use the **arrow buttons** underneath to show **more answer options**.

Putting New Words in Context

Try some sentence-level games

True or false?

In this **listening game**, you hear a question and a response. You have to say whether the response you hear is "**vrai**" ("true") or "**faux**" ("false"), depending on whether or not it matches the **image** on the screen.

What's the answer?

This is another **listening game**, but this time it's about **picking out** the correct **form** of response to a question. You hear a question and three possible answers — two of which are answering a **completely different question**.

Listen and match

This final **listening game** combines vocabulary from the lesson with **colours**, **numbers** and other **basic adjectives**.

Make a sentence

This simple **word game** tests how well pupils remember **sentence structures**. You have to **rearrange** muddled-up words to make a sentence.

What are they saying?

This one's a **reading game**. Read the sentence in the speech bubble and **choose** the image that matches it.

Song Lessons

Each unit has a **song** lesson — it's usually the **first lesson** of the unit.
Song lessons have all the **same features** as a normal lesson, **plus** a song.

French karaoke

Sing along with the songs in French using the **karaoke** screen.
Use the **lyrics** to help your class learn the words.

See what's coming next

The **next line** of the song is shown **faintly** on top of the picture, so you're ready for it when it comes.

Sing with or without the singer

Once pupils are familiar with the song, you can **turn off the vocals** to see how much they've learnt.

Show or hide the words

Show the French and/or English lyrics to help pupils sing along, or **hide** both French and English to see what they remember.

There are also printable song lyrics for every song (see p.21), showing the French and English.

Classroom Tips

- Play the song through to the class first with the French **and** English lyrics showing, to help them **understand** the words and get used to the **tune**.

- As they sing along, you could ask your class to come up with **actions** to make the song more **fun** and **memorable**.

- Consider coming **back** to the song later in the unit to reinforce learning.

Story Lessons

At the **end** of each unit, there's a **story** lesson. This story draws together some of the vocabulary learnt earlier in the unit. (For some units, the text will be a **recipe** or other activity instead of an actual story, but the lesson works in the same way.)

> **Classroom Tips**
>
> - There are no new **question and answer** structures (see p.12) in story lessons, so you can focus on **tying together** what you've covered in the unit so far.
> - Before starting the story, you might want to play some quick games to **remind** your class of the language they learnt earlier in the unit — you'll find **suggested activities** in the **Scheme of Work** document (see p.26).
> - You might want to look at the **printable version** of the story too (see p.22).

Move at the class's pace

Control the speed of the story by using the arrows to **move** to the next page.

Or use the **dots** to skip to a particular place in the story.

Show French or English

Choose to show the French text, English text or both, to suit your class.

Listen in French

Click on the 'Listen' button to hear the story **read out loud** in French.

Auto Play

You can 'Start Auto Play' to **see** and **hear** the story played right through. Click the button **again** at any time to **pause** the story.

The Printable Lesson Resources

Finding your Resources

There are two ways to get to your **printable lesson resources**, through a lesson's '**Overview & Resources**' (see p.6) or through '**Teacher Resources**'.

Opening from the Lesson Overview

This is the easiest way to find all the resources for a **particular lesson**.

Find the lesson you want using the main menu and expand the lesson's '**Overview & Resources**', here.

Select a resource from the table to **open** it in Adobe® PDF format. You can then **print** it as normal.

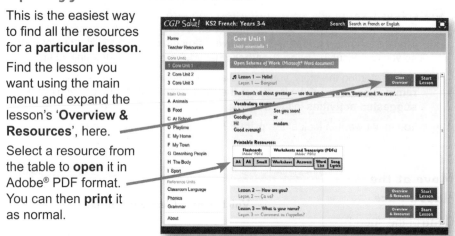

Opening from Teacher Resources

If you want to **browse** resources, or print worksheets and flashcards for **several lessons at once**, you might find it easier to go through '**Teacher Resources**'.

Click on '**Teacher Resources**' at the top of the unit list.

In '**Printable Lesson Resources by Unit**' you'll find this table, which shows all the resources for a whole unit.

Choose the **unit** you want from the list on the left.

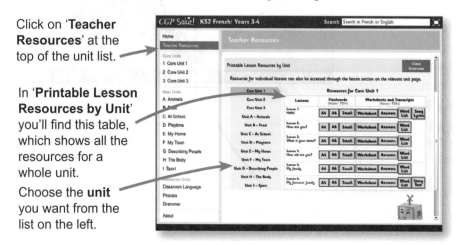

Worksheets

There's a **printable worksheet** for every lesson. They contain fun **activities**, and suggest **additional exercises** for more confident children.

Print out and fill in

Each worksheet contains **simple reading** and **writing** activities to help **consolidate** the vocabulary and sentence structures learnt in the lesson.

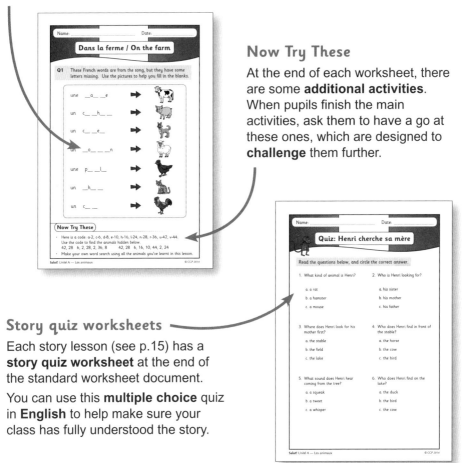

Now Try These

At the end of each worksheet, there are some **additional activities**. When pupils finish the main activities, ask them to have a go at these ones, which are designed to **challenge** them further.

Story quiz worksheets

Each story lesson (see p.15) has a **story quiz worksheet** at the end of the standard worksheet document.

You can use this **multiple choice** quiz in **English** to help make sure your class has fully understood the story.

Worksheet answers

Salut! also has **answers** for all the **worksheets** and **quizzes** so you can mark pupils' work quickly and confidently.

Flashcards

All of the lessons in *Salut!* have **flashcards** to print and use with your class. The flashcards come in **three sizes** — **A4**, **A6** and **small**.

A4

Print out the **image flashcards** in **A4** to play flashcard games with the **whole class**. They're **big** enough that everyone will be able to see them.

These **large images** can be great for **wall displays** too.

A6

The **A6 image flashcards** are great for playing flashcard games in **small groups**.

Small

These ones are effectively **two sets** of cards — **image** cards and **text** cards.

You can make **double-sided flashcards** by cutting along the horizontal dotted lines only and folding the text behind the image along this line.

Flashcards

Flashcard activities

Show me... / Montrez-moi...

Hand out a selection of **flashcards** to your class. Call out simple sentences like "**Montrez-moi les pommes!**" ("Show me the apples!"). The pupil who has a picture of the apples on their flashcard should **hold it up** to show you and the rest of the class. Replace "*les pommes*" in the sentence with **other items of vocabulary** on the flashcards.

Bingo

Cut out the small flashcards to make some **bingo cards** with **pictures** on them. Then put the matching **word cards** in a bag to draw from. You could call the bingo yourself, or for an added challenge, ask for **volunteers** to draw a card from the bag and read it to the class.

Pairs

Use the **small** flashcards to make a simple pairs game. In pairs, pupils lay the **picture** cards face-down in **one row** and the **word** cards face-down in **another row**. They then take turns to turn over **one** card from each row. If the cards **match**, that player keeps them and has another turn. The winner is the player with most cards at the end.

Word Lists

For each lesson, you can print a list of the **vocabulary** in English and French.

Pupils can build their own 'dictionary'

These sheets contain a list of all the **vocabulary** in a lesson, and chosen **examples** from the 'Question & Answer' screen. Your class can use them to build their own English-French **dictionary** by topic.

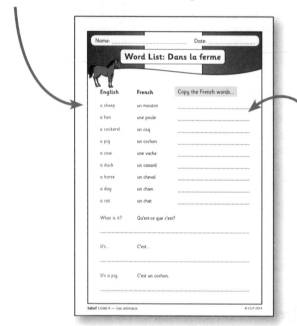

Space to practise

There's space for pupils to **copy** out the French words to help them **learn** the vocabulary and develop their **spelling** in French.

Classroom Tips

- If a child needs a reminder of the written French, e.g. for one of the **worksheet** activities (see p.17), try giving them a copy of the word list with the **English covered** or folded underneath.

- Encourage your class to use the **question and answer** section at the bottom of the sheet as a **model** for their own sentences.

- Copying out the French might feel like a **dull** exercise, but many children will find it helps the words to stick in their heads. You could consider setting it as a **homework** exercise.

Song Lyrics

There are **printable versions** of all the **song lyrics**, with **English translations**.

French with English translations

All of the songs are **translated** into English so pupils can see the French and English **side-by-side**.

| Classroom Tips |

As an extension activity for more confident pupils, try this **translation** task:

- Ask them to look at the text and find the **French equivalent** of an English phrase (or vice versa). This should be a phrase they **haven't** actively been taught yet.

- So in this example, you could ask them to find the French for "*a farm*" and "*I live*". Or ask them to work out what "*il y a*" means in English.

- **Be careful** with prepositions like "in" and "on", though. The French doesn't always use the same word as the English. So, in this case, the French "*dans*" literally translates to "*in*". But in English, we say "*on a farm*" not "*in a farm*". If in doubt, check a **dictionary** — there are some good ones online that give you plenty of examples to make the meaning clear.

22

Story Texts

To go with the **story lessons** (p.15), there are printable versions of the story text in both French and English.

French with English translations

In the story text Adobe® PDF document, you'll find a **French page** and a separate **English page.**

| Classroom Tips |

You can use the **French** version of the story text to do a **warm-up** activity at the beginning of your story lesson:

- Ask pupils to **point out** any words they **recognise** in the text, before you start reading. See if they can remember what the words mean.

- This is a good **revision activity** and a good exercise in identifying **key words** in a text. It can also make the story feel less **daunting**.

Finding your Documents

If you click on '**Teacher Resources**' at the top of the unit list on the main menu, you'll get a screen a bit like the one below:

Click on the **blue buttons** on the right to expand these **Overviews**.

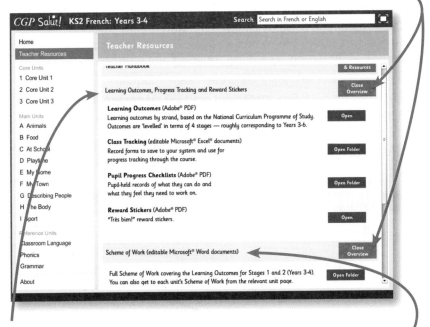

Learning Outcomes, Progress Tracking and Reward Stickers

In this section, you'll find documents for tracking your class's progress against the **National Curriculum Programme of Study**.

There's a full set of measurable **learning outcomes** (see next page), a **summary** tracking sheet (see p.25), and a self-assessment **checklist** for pupils to fill in (see p.25).

There's also a set of **printable reward stickers** made with images of the top prizes from the CGP Prize-o-matic (see p.11).

Scheme of Work

From here, you can open a folder containing all the **Scheme of Work** documents (see p.26) in Microsoft® Word format.

These are the **same** documents that you can open from each unit on the **main menu** screen (see p.6), but we've stuck them all together here for easy reference.

Learning Outcomes

The KS2 Programme of Study for foreign languages can be a little **daunting**. So we've put together a set of **measurable Learning Outcomes** to make the whole process of making and recording progress a bit more manageable.

Learning Outcomes are split by strand and Stage (Year)

The KS2 Programme of Study contains **12 statements** covering the full four years of study. We've broken these PoS statements down into four strands — **listening**, **speaking**, **reading** and **writing**.

Each learning outcome uses a concrete '*I can...*' format.

The outcomes for each PoS statement gradually **increase in difficulty** — giving you an **attainment ladder** for measuring progress.

Full PoS statements

Learning Outcomes are **colour-coded** by Stage (Year) for easy reference.

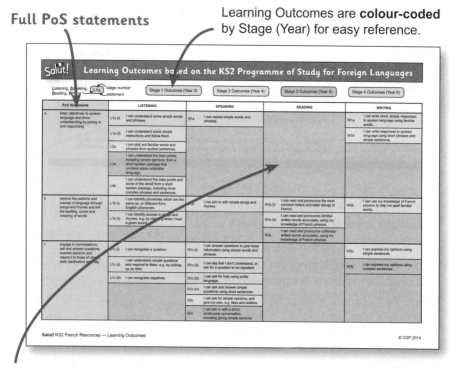

The Learning Outcomes are in the main body of the table

Some cells in the table are **empty**, because not every PoS statement applies to every strand. E.g. there are no **reading** outcomes for statement **a**.

Progress Tracking

There are two documents in '**Teacher Resources**' to help you **track progress**.

Class Tracking — for summative teacher assessment

There's one of these forms for each Stage of *Salut!*,
so you can **keep track** of how your class is doing.

Summary statements by strand

Along the top there are **summary statements** for each strand, describing
what you should **expect** a pupil to be able to do by the **end** of the stage.

		Class Tracking Form — Stage 1		
	Listening: Can recognise questions and negatives. Can understand and respond to simple instructions and questions. Can identify sounds in the French language. Can recognise some adjectives, and identify plurals in spoken French.	**Speaking:** Can join in with simple songs and rhymes. Can ask and answer simple questions using accurate pronunciation, so that others can understand them. Can talk about themselves using some common verbs in the first person singular form.	**Reading:** Can read and pronounce familiar written words accurately. Can understand familiar written phrases and simple sentences, and respond to them. Can recognise whether written nouns are singular or plural.	**Writing:** Can write some familiar words from memory. Can write short, simple responses to questions using familiar words. Can write some singular nouns with the correct article.

Name | Checkpoint 1 / Checkpoint 2 | Achieved? (Yes, Almost, No) | ...

'Checkpoints' for termly assessment

You can use the **checkpoint** boxes to track a pupil's progress at several points in the year (e.g. the end of each term).

> If you've got a fairly up-to-date version of Microsoft® Excel®, this spreadsheet will **auto-format**. Just type 'y' for yes, 'a' for almost or 'n' for no and the **colouring** will be added automatically.

Pupil Progress Checklists

Encourage pupils to keep a **record** of what they can do using a **Pupil Progress Checklist**.

This checklist contains all the '*I can...*' learning outcomes for the stage they're working at.

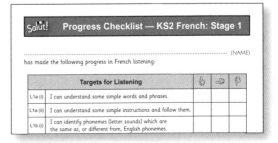

Salut! **Progress Checklist — KS2 French: Stage 1**

.... (NAME)

has made the following progress in French listening:

	Targets for Listening			
L1a (i)	I can understand some simple words and phrases.			
L1a (ii)	I can understand some simple instructions and follow them.			
L1b (i)	I can identify phonemes (letter sounds) which are the same as, or different from, English phonemes.			

Scheme of Work Documents

For each unit, there's a detailed **Scheme of Work** document to help you plan engaging lessons for your class.

Unit Overview

The first page of the Scheme of Work document is a unit **overview**.

Introduction to the unit

This **quick** introduction gives you an instant feel for what the unit's about and how it **fits** with the rest of the course. It includes a list of **useful prior knowledge** and a summary of the **new language content**.

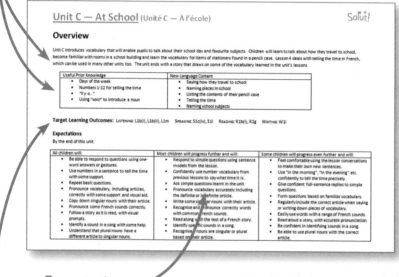

Expectations

Gauge your class's progress against these **expectations**. The second column corresponds to the skill level of the Target Learning Outcomes.

Target Learning Outcomes

These **codes** refer to the **Learning Outcomes** table (see p.24). These are the **skills** that this unit focuses on. Different units have different focuses, but all the learning outcomes are covered at least once over the course of the Scheme of Work.

Scheme of Work Documents

Weekly Plan

The rest of the document is the **Weekly Plan** — use this to help you structure and plan your lessons. The Weekly Plans are **fully editable** in Microsoft® Word, so you can **customise** them with your own notes and activity ideas.

Familiarise yourself with the language content

The **key vocabulary** for the lesson is listed here. These are the words covered in '**Present Vocab**' and '**Review Vocab**' (see pages 8-9).

You can also see the **question** and a **model** for the **answer**, that appear on the lesson's '**Question and Answer**' screen (see p.12).

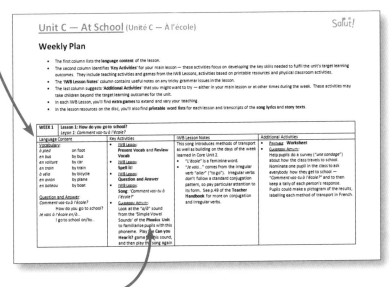

Key Activities

The second column lists '**Key Activities**' for your main lesson — these activities focus on developing the skills needed to fulfil the unit's Target Learning Outcomes (see previous page). They include teaching activities and games from the **IWB lessons**, activities based on **printable resources** and physical **classroom activities**.

> I've run out of room here, but there's more on the next page.

Scheme of Work Documents

IWB Lesson Notes

Although we've tried to create lessons with **simple** vocabulary and sentence structures, inevitably technical points *do* crop up. These notes explain any **quirks**, and point out situations where the French is different from the English in ways you might not expect.

Where there are specific **grammatical** issues, we point you in the direction of the relevant pages in the second half of **this Handbook**.

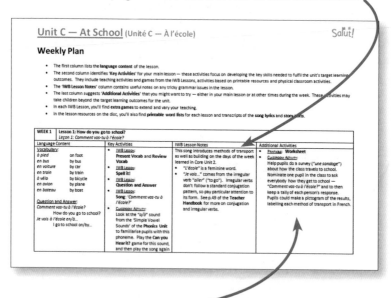

Additional Activities

The last column suggests '**Additional Activities**' that you might want to try — either in your main lesson or at other times during the week.

These activities will sometimes take children **beyond** the target learning outcomes for the unit, so they might not be appropriate for all members of your class.

Whole Unit Activities

At the **end** of the document, you'll find some suggestions for activities that use language from across the unit. These can be useful for end-of-unit lessons, or **mid-unit** revision activities.

Classroom Language Unit

'**Classroom Language**' introduces some useful classroom words and phrases that will help your class to **speak in French** as much as possible.

Talk in French whenever you can

The idea of this unit is to introduce your class to lots of **common classroom words** and **phrases** which you can use in your lessons.

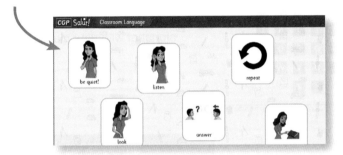

Introduce useful little words...

Introduce some **basic useful words**, such as "**oui**" ("yes") and "**non**" ("no") to get your pupils started.

...and useful little phrases

The last set of vocabulary is a bit **trickier**, so you might want to save that for when your class is a little more **confident** with the language.

Classroom Tips

- Make a **wall display** of all the classroom instructions for the children to refer to — then you can use them in your lessons as much as possible.

- Encourage the children to use the useful words and phrases when they want to say or ask something during your French lessons.

- For example, "merci" ("thank you"), "pourquoi?" ("why?"), "Je ne comprends pas" ("I don't understand") or "Qu'est-ce que c'est?" ("What is it?").

Phonics Unit

The **Phonics Unit** is a great starting point for developing good French **pronunciation** — it covers some **important French sounds**.

Sounds of the alphabet

Hear the **alphabet** pronounced in French. Practise reciting the alphabet with your class.

Tricky sounds

Click on a **sound** to hear how it's pronounced in French.

Sounds in context

Once you've listened to the isolated sound, listen to it in the **context** of the **example words**.

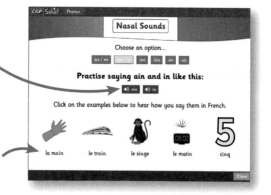

Practise with simple games

When your class has listened to some sounds, let them **practise** their understanding by playing the phonics games — '**Can you hear it?**' and '**Can you spell it?**'.

Grammar Unit

The **Grammar Unit** is the last of the three **Reference Units** included in *Salut!*. You can use it to teach pupils the **basics** of **French grammar**. (There are some more comprehensive grammar notes for **you** in the second half of this book.)

Reference tool

French grammar can be a bit **intimidating**.

The Grammar Unit explains some basics of French grammar, such as **adjective agreement** and **verb conjugation**, in a simple, example-led way.

It's designed as a **reference tool**, so you can **dip into** it whenever you like.

Choose a **section** and a **topic** from the Grammar menu to start.

Interactive glossary

Click on the **question mark** to see a **definition** of the underlined term.

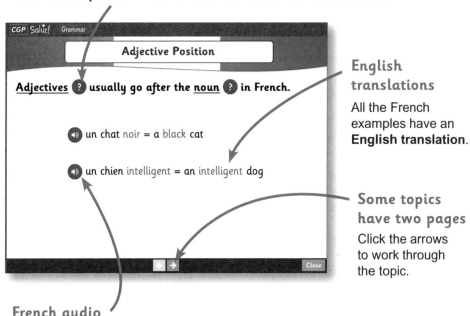

English translations

All the French examples have an **English translation**.

Some topics have two pages

Click the arrows to work through the topic.

French audio

Click on the audio button next to an **example** to hear it read **out loud**. Encourage pupils to **repeat** what they hear.

General Activity Ideas

There are lots of lesson-specific activities in the Scheme of Work, but here are some **ideas for general activities** that you can try with your class at any time.

You'll find some general **flashcard-based activities** on page 19 too.

Simple lesson starters

These activities practise some of the language from the **Core Units** and the **Classroom Language** Unit. But they're really intended to help your class get into a **French mood** at the start of each lesson.

The attendance register / Le registre de présence

Ask pupils to answer the **register** with "*Bonjour, Monsieur!*" ("Hello, sir!") or "*Bonjour, Madame!*" ("Hello, madam!") to get them speaking in French right from the start of the lesson.

The date / La date

At the beginning of each lesson, ask "*Quelle est la date d'aujourd'hui?*" ("What is the date today?") or "*On est quel jour?*" ("What day is it?")

Ask one pupil to write the **day of the week**, another to write the **number** and a third to write the **month**, on the board.

If you class isn't confident **writing** the French, you could ask for a volunteer to **tell you** what to write instead.

Simon says / Jacques a dit

This traditional game can be played with vocabulary from the **Classroom Language** Unit, like "*Levez la main!*" ("Raise your hand!").

You could extend the game by asking pupils to touch (*"touchez"*) different **parts of their body**, or **mime the actions** for other activities, e.g. from the **daily routine** and **sports** lessons.

Classroom Tips
Playing a game like 'Simon says' for a few minutes at the start of a lesson can help the children to **relax** and 'get their ear in'.

General Activity Ideas

General teaching activities

The rest of the **general activities** on these pages are less **content-specific**, so you can use them for lots of different topics.

- There's a mixture of **whole class activities, group activities** and **individual tasks**.
- There are **listening, speaking** and **reading** activities, so you can choose one that uses the skills you're focussing on.

What is it? / Qu'est-ce que c'est?

This is a simple **speaking** activity.

Point to an object in the room, on the board or on a flashcard and ask "**Qu'est-ce que c'est?**" ("What is it?").

Encourage pupils to reply in full sentences, for example, "**C'est une chaise.**" ("It's a chair."). With the more confident children in your class, ask them to give as much detail as they can, e.g. "**C'est une chaise bleue.**" ("It's a blue chair.").

Question or statement? / Question ou déclaration?

This is a simple **listening** activity for the whole class.

Ask each child to write a **full stop** on one side of a piece of paper or whiteboard, and a question mark on the other.

Then call out a selection of **statements** from the topic you're working on.
Make some of the statements into **questions** by **raising the tone of your voice at the end**.

Ask pupils to hold up the **correct punctuation mark** to match the sentence.

General Activity Ideas

Find... / Trouvez...

This is a great activity for practising **adjectives** and **listening skills**.

Ask a pupil to, e.g. *"Trouvez un objet vert dans la salle de classe."* ("Find a green object in the classroom.") *"Vert"* ("green") can be replaced with other **colours** or **adjectives** that the class is familiar with.

Classroom Tips

- This activity can also work well for finding things in a **book** or **catalogue**.
- In this case, you would just say, *"Trouvez un objet vert."*
- Using pictures in a book rather than physical objects gives you a wider range of vocabulary to play with.

Charades / Un jeu de mime

This game works particularly well with lessons on **sport** and **daily routine**.

Get pupils to take turns **miming an action**. The rest of the class must **correctly guess** what the mime is in **French**. To make the game more **competitive**, split the class into **teams**, and award points for correct answers.

Four corners / Les quatre coins

This activity can get a bit raucous, so it's a good one to play outside or in the sports hall. You'll need to split your class into **teams**.

Stick some large pictures up around the hall or playground to create 'stations'. Place matching word or sentence cards face-down on the floor, roughly equal distances away from each station.

One player from each team chooses a card. When you clap your hands, they all turn over their cards, read them and run to the matching station. The first player to reach the right station is the winner.

This is a **reading** version of the classic 'stations' game, but you can play similar games to practise listening skills. E.g. everyone stands in the middle of the hall. You call out a phrase in French and they all have to run to the matching station.

General Activity Ideas

Repeat if it's true / Répétez si c'est vrai

This is an exercise in **listening** and **repetition**. Tell pupils that they have to "*Répétez si c'est vrai!*" ("Repeat if it's true!").

Either using a set of flashcards or physical objects, point to one and say a simple sentence about it, e.g. "*C'est un stylo.*" ("It's a pen.") or "*C'est bleu.*" ("It's blue."). Some of these statements should be **true**, and some **false**. Pupils should **repeat** the **true** statements, but **stay silent** if they're **false**.

For more confident children, try using more **complex** statements, e.g. "*C'est un stylo bleu.*" ("It's a blue pen.")

Chinese whispers / Le téléphone arabe

This game is good for practising **speaking** and **listening** skills.

Arrange the children in lines with about six children in each line. At the end of the lines should be a table containing either a set of **picture flashcards** or **physical objects**.

Give the child at the other end of each line a card with a **written sentence** on it, e.g. "*J'ai deux pommes.*" ("I have two apples.") They must whisper it to the second child, who whispers it to the next child and so on down the line. The last person in the line must pick up the matching object from the table.

The first team to pick up the matching object from the table wins.

Is it a...? / C'est un...?

In this game, you **draw an object** on the board one line at a time, and the class have to guess what it is you're drawing.

After each line, stop and ask the class "*Qu'est-ce que c'est?*" ("What is it?"). Encourage your class to respond with a guess in the form of a **question**, e.g. "*C'est une table?*" by raising the tone of their voice at the end of the sentence.

You can also get children to play this game **in pairs** on a mini whiteboard.

General Activity Ideas

Role-play / Jeu de rôle

Pupils can make up a **role-play** conversation using the **question and answer** they've learnt in a lesson, together with greetings and polite language from other units.

This activity works really well with **shop scenarios**, and you could even set up a pretend shop in class. The 'shopkeeper' should say "*Qu'est-ce que vous désirez?*" ("What would you like?") and the 'customer' can use "*Je voudrais..., s'il vous plaît.*" ("I would like..., please.") to reply.

A puppet show / Un spectacle de marionnettes

It can be fun to make **puppets** of **characters** from the stories. When they're complete, encourage children to give a **puppet show** using their puppets and a **printout of the story** to help them.

A survey / Un sondage

Ask pupils to write down **questions** that they've learnt during the lesson. More confident pupils might be able to **invent new questions** based on the question structures learnt in class.

Get pupils to ask the rest of the class the questions in French and keep a **tally** of the responses. Encourage respondents to answer in **full French sentences**. The children could then make **charts** from the class's findings to display on the wall.

What's the time, Mr Wolf? / Quelle heure est-il, Monsieur Loup?

This activity isn't strictly content-free, but it's a fun game to practise **numbers** and **telling the time**. One pupil is the '**wolf**' and stands facing a wall. The rest of the children creep closer to the wolf by asking what time it is — "*Quelle heure est-il, Monsieur Loup?*" — and then taking the appropriate number of steps depending on the wolf's reply, e.g. "*Il est deux heures*" = **two** steps. The wolf then calls "*Il est l'heure de vous manger!*" ("It's time to eat you!") and chases the pupils back to the start line. The first pupil to be caught is the new wolf.

Articles

This second half of the book is a basic guide to French grammar and punctuation, aimed at non-specialists. Use it as a **reference tool**, or spend a bit of time swotting up to stay well **ahead of your class**.

Gender and articles

- Every French noun is either **masculine** or **feminine**.
- You can usually tell a noun's gender from its **article** (see below).
- If you're **unsure** of a noun's gender, you can check by looking the word up in a **bilingual dictionary**.
- French nouns usually **need** an article. Sometimes the article is **combined with a preposition** (see pages 38-40), but as a rule it shouldn't be left out, even if it doesn't appear in the English.

J'aime le tennis. ⟶ I like (the) tennis.

Definite articles

The word you use for "the" depends on whether the noun is **masculine, feminine, plural** or starts with a **vowel**.

Masculine singular	Feminine singular	In front of a vowel, or silent "*h*"	Masculine or feminine plural
le	la	l'	les

le chien — the dog   la pomme — the apple
l'oiseau — the bird   les pommes — the apples

Indefinite articles

- There are two words for "a" in French.
- "*Un*" is used for singular **masculine** nouns.
- "*Une*" is used for singular **feminine** nouns.

un chien (a dog)

une vache (a cow)

The indefinite article for plural nouns is "*des*" ("some").

Prepositions — 'à'

French prepositions, just like English ones, come before nouns and pronouns to express a **relationship**, e.g. *at, by, from, under*, etc.

The complication comes when they're **combined** with an article.

Definite articles with "à"

"*à*" means "at" or "to". If you want to say "at the" or "to the", "*à*" **combines** with the definite article like this:

$$à + le = au \qquad à + la = à \, la$$
$$à + l' = à \, l' \qquad à + les = aux$$

il est à + le marché ⟶ Il est au marché. (He's at the market.)

je vais à + la piscine ⟶ Je vais à la piscine. (I go to the swimming pool.)

je suis à + l'hôpital ⟶ Je suis à l'hôpital. (I'm at the hospital.)

je vais à + les magasins ⟶ Je vais aux magasins. (I go to the shops.)

"*à*" can also follow certain verbs, such as "*jouer*" ("to play"). It combines with "*le*", "*la*" or "*les*" in exactly the same way.

je joue à + le foot ⟶ Je joue au foot. (I play football.)

Remember that the article can't be left out in French even though it doesn't appear in the English.

je joue à + la balle ⟶ Je joue à la balle. (I play catch.)

je joue à + les jeux vidéo ⟶ Je joue aux jeux vidéo. (I play video games.)

"*Jouer*" isn't always followed by "*à*". When you're talking about playing a musical instrument, it takes the preposition "*de*" — see p.40.

Prepositions — 'de'

Another **very** common preposition is "*de*". It crops up an awful lot in French, so read these pages to find out more.

Definite articles with "de"

- "*De*" can mean "**any**", "**some**" or "**of**".
- When "*de*" is used before a noun, it **combines** with the **article** in the following ways.

> de + le = du   de + la = de la
> de + l' = de l'   de + les = des

Je mange du fromage. (I'm eating some cheese.)

> If you said "*Je mange le fromage.*" it would mean "I'm eating the cheese." — as in a specific piece of cheese rather than some cheese in general.

Le nord de la France. (The north of France.)

Tu as de l'ananas? (Do you have any pineapple?)

Tu as des frites? (Do you have any chips?)

"De" can also mean "from"

Je suis de Paris. (I am from Paris.)

C'est un cadeau de ma mère. (It's a present from my mother.)

Prepositions — 'de'

"De" after verbs

- "*De*" also **follows** certain verbs.
- "*Faire*" ("to do") and "*jouer*" ("to play") are often followed by "*de*". "*De*" combines with "*le*", "*la*" or "*les*" in exactly the same way as when it's used after a definite article.

J'aime faire de la natation. (I like swimming.)

J'aime faire de l'escalade. (I like climbing.)

Je joue du saxophone. (I play the saxophone.)

Sometimes "*jouer*" is followed by "*à*" — see p.38.

Je joue des cymbales. (I play the cymbals.)

When "de" doesn't change

Sometimes, "*de*" **replaces** the article — so it **doesn't change**.

1. When you're saying "*beaucoup de*" ("lots of").

   J'ai beaucoup de cadeaux. (I have lots of presents.)

2. When you're using "*de*" with a **specific quantity**.

   15 g de farine (15 g of flour)

3. In a **negative** sentence.

   Je ne mange pas de pizza. (I don't eat pizza.)

   See p.56 for more about negative sentences.

   Je n'ai pas d'animaux. (I don't have any animals.)

   An apostrophe replaces the "*e*" in "*de*" here to avoid two vowels being next to each other — see p.55 for more.

Plurals

There are some simple rules for making French nouns plural.

Usually you just add an "s"

To make **most nouns** plural in French, you simply add an "**s**".

le chien (the dog) ⟶ les chiens (the dogs)

> Don't forget that the article ("*le*") will also change from singular to plural — see p.37.

But there are some exceptions

• Words that end in "s", "x" or "z" usually **stay the same**:

le bras (the arm) ⟶ les bras (the arms)

• Nouns ending in "*eau*" or "*eu*" usually just need an "**x**" to become plural:

l'oiseau (the bird) ⟶ les oiseaux (the birds)

le jeu (the game) ⟶ les jeux (the games)

• If a noun ends in "*al*", it normally changes to "***aux***" when it becomes plural.

le cheval (the horse) ⟶ les chevaux (the horses)

l'animal (the animal) ⟶ les animaux (the animals)

• Some plurals don't follow a pattern — you just have to **learn them**:

> You usually add an "*s*" to nouns ending in "*ou*" to make them plural — "*les bijoux*" is an exception.

l'œil (the eye) ⟶ les yeux (the eyes)

le bijou (the jewel) ⟶ les bijoux (the jewels / the jewellery)

Adjectives

Adjectives, including colours, are a little complicated in French.

Adjectives must agree with the noun

- Most adjectives have a masculine and feminine version — you should use the version that **agrees** with the **noun** they describe.

> Adjectives on the 'Present Vocab' screens are usually in their masculine singular form.

- Usually, you add an "**e**" to make an adjective **feminine**.

le vélo bleu (the blue bicycle)   la voiture bleue (the blue car)

- Adjectives also have **plural** versions. Plural versions are usually made by adding an "**s**" to the end of the singular versions.

les vélos bleus (the blue bicycles)   les voitures bleues (the blue cars)

Irregular adjectives

- Some adjectives are irregular and **don't follow the rules** above.
- Here are some of the most common irregular adjectives:

English	Masculine singular	Feminine singular	Masculine plural	Feminine plural
beautiful	beau*	belle	beaux	belles
old	vieux**	vieille	vieux	vieilles
new	nouveau***	nouvelle	nouveaux	nouvelles
friendly	gentil	gentille	gentils	gentilles
boring	ennuyeux	ennuyeuse	ennuyeux	ennuyeuses
white	blanc	blanche	blancs	blanches
purple	violet	violette	violets	violettes
all	tout	toute	tous	toutes

* *"bel"* before a vowel or a silent *h*.   ** *"vieil"* before a vowel or a silent *h*.
*** *"nouvel"* before a vowel or a silent *h*.

Adjectives

Adjectives that don't change

- There are a few adjectives that always **stay the same**, whether the noun they're modifying is masculine, feminine or plural.

- These are words that are also **nouns** in their own right.

- For example, "*marron*" ("brown") can also mean "a chestnut" ("*un marron*"), so it **doesn't change** when it's being used as an adjective.

Even though "*les yeux*" is plural, "*marron*" doesn't change. → les yeux marron (the brown eyes)

- Other colours that are used in the same way are "*rose*" ("pink" / "a rose"), "*orange*" ("orange" / "an orange") and "*noisette*" ("hazel" / "a hazelnut").

The position of adjectives

- French adjectives usually come **after** the noun.

une pomme verte (a green apple)

- But there are some adjectives that can come **before** the noun. Here are the most common ones:

Adjective	English
beau / belle / bel / beaux / belles	handsome / beautiful
nouveau / nouvelle / nouvel / nouveaux / nouvelles	new
petit / petite / petits / petites	small
mauvais / mauvaise / mauvais / mauvaises	nasty
jeune / jeunes	young
vieux / vieille / vieil / vieux / vieilles	old

Comparatives and Adverbs

Here are three more ways to describe in French.

Comparatives

To form comparatives, you just need to remember the words "**plus**" (more), "**moins**" (less) and "**que**" (than).

Le troll est plus âgé que la princesse. (The troll is older than the princess.)

La momie est plus jolie que le pirate. (The mummy is prettier than the pirate.)

"jolie" has an extra "e" here to make it feminine to agree with "la momie".

Remember that the adjective still needs to agree with the noun you're describing.

Superlatives

- If you want to say that something is "the most", just put "**le plus**" / "**la plus**" in front of the adjective.

Elle est la plus jeune de sa classe. (She is the youngest in her class.)

- To say "the least", you need to use "**le moins**" / "**la moins**" in front of the adjective.

C'est le moins célèbre de ses livres. (It is the least famous of his books.)

Adverbs

- Many French adverbs are formed by adding "**ment**" to the end of the feminine form of the adjective.

lent (slow) (m) ⟶ lente (slow) (f) ⟶ lentement (slowly)

- Adverbs **don't change** to agree with the gender or number of the noun.

Possessive Adjectives

'Possessive adjective' is just the technical term for a word like 'my' or 'his'.

Possessive adjectives

- As with other adjectives in French, possessive adjectives **agree** with the **object** (the noun), not the subject (the person the object belongs to).

- So they change depending on the **gender** of the **noun**, and whether the noun is **singular** or **plural**.

	Masculine singular	Feminine singular	Plural
my	mon	ma	mes
your	ton	ta	tes
his / her / its	son	sa	ses
our	notre	notre	nos
your	votre	votre	vos
their	leur	leur	leurs

Here are some examples of possessive adjectives in **context**:

Mon lapin aime les carottes. (My rabbit likes carrots.)

J'aime ton chapeau. (I like your hat.)

C'est sa voiture. (It's his/her car.) ◄—— This could mean "his car" or "her car" because "sa" agrees with "voiture" ("car"), which is feminine. It never agrees with the person that owns the car (the subject).

Exception

If the possessive adjective for a singular noun comes before a word that begins with a vowel, you **always** use the masculine form.

Elle est ton amie? (Is she your friend?)

Son idée est intéressante. (His/her idea is interesting.)

"Ta amie" or "sa idée" would be awkward to say.

Pronouns

Subject pronouns

Subject pronouns are used in the same way as in English — they **replace** the **subject** of the sentence (the person or thing **doing** the action).

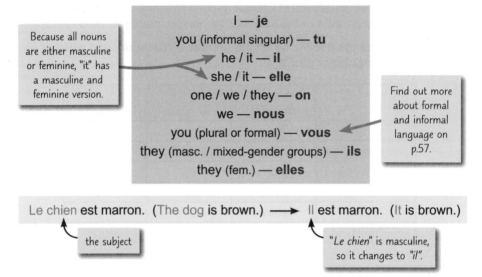

Because all nouns are either masculine or feminine, "it" has a masculine and feminine version.

I — **je**
you (informal singular) — **tu**
he / it — **il**
she / it — **elle**
one / we / they — **on**
we — **nous**
you (plural or formal) — **vous**
they (masc. / mixed-gender groups) — **ils**
they (fem.) — **elles**

Find out more about formal and informal language on p.57.

Le chien **est marron.** (The dog is brown.) ⟶ Il **est marron.** (It is brown.)

the subject

"*Le chien*" is masculine, so it changes to "*il*".

Direct object pronouns

Direct object pronouns **replace** the **direct object** of a sentence (the person or thing that the action is **being done to**).

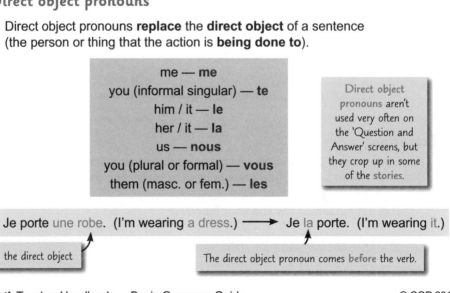

me — **me**
you (informal singular) — **te**
him / it — **le**
her / it — **la**
us — **nous**
you (plural or formal) — **vous**
them (masc. or fem.) — **les**

Direct object pronouns aren't used very often on the 'Question and Answer' screens, but they crop up in some of the stories.

Je porte une robe. (I'm wearing a dress.) ⟶ Je la porte. (I'm wearing it.)

the direct object

The direct object pronoun comes before the verb.

Reflexive Pronouns

Reflexive pronouns

- **Reflexive pronouns** refer to the self, e.g. "myself", "yourself", "himself", etc. We don't use reflexives very much in English, but they're a little more common in French.

- The **infinitive** forms of some verbs in French have the reflexive pronoun "**se**" before them — these are **reflexive** verbs.
  E.g. "*se cacher*" ("to hide [oneself]") and "*s'appeler*" ("to be called").

- In French, reflexive verbs have a **reflexive pronoun** directly in front of them — you use the one that **matches** the **subject pronoun**.

> myself — **me**
> yourself (informal singular) — **te**
> oneself / himself / herself / itself — **se**
> ourselves — **nous**
> yourself (formal) / yourselves — **vous**
> themselves — **se**

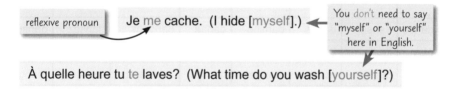

reflexive pronoun   Je me cache. (I hide [myself].) ← You don't need to say "myself" or "yourself" here in English.

À quelle heure tu te laves? (What time do you wash [yourself]?)

Watch out for verbs beginning with a **vowel** or a **silent "h"**:

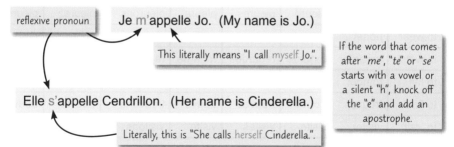

reflexive pronoun   Je m'appelle Jo. (My name is Jo.)

This literally means "I call myself Jo.".

Elle s'appelle Cendrillon. (Her name is Cinderella.)

Literally, this is "She calls herself Cinderella.".

If the word that comes after "*me*", "*te*" or "*se*" starts with a vowel or a silent "h", knock off the "e" and add an apostrophe.

Verbs

Here are some common verbs in the present tense.

Verbs in the present tense

- French verbs change depending on the **subject** (who is doing the action).

J'aime les chats. (I like cats.) ⟶ Tu aimes les chats. (You like cats.)

- Like English verbs, French verbs can be **regular** or **irregular**.

Regular verbs

Here are some **regular** verbs used in *Salut!* — they're in the **present** tense. These verbs all end with "er", so the **conjugations** all follow the **same** pattern.

English	Infinitive (to ...)	je / j'	tu	il / elle / on	nous	vous	ils / elles
to like	aimer	aime	aimes	aime	aimons	aimez	aiment
to sing	chanter	chante	chantes	chante	chantons	chantez	chantent
to look for	chercher	cherche	cherches	cherche	cherchons	cherchez	cherchent
to dance	danser	danse	danses	danse	dansons	dansez	dansent
to play	jouer	joue	joues	joue	jouons	jouez	jouent
to eat	manger	mange	manges	mange	mangeons*	mangez	mangent
to walk	marcher	marche	marches	marche	marchons	marchez	marchent
to talk	parler	parle	parles	parle	parlons	parlez	parlent
to cry	pleurer	pleure	pleures	pleure	pleurons	pleurez	pleurent
to wear	porter	porte	portes	porte	portons	portez	portent
to watch	regarder	regarde	regardes	regarde	regardons	regardez	regardent
to fall	tomber	tombe	tombes	tombe	tombons	tombez	tombent
to find	trouver	trouve	trouves	trouve	trouvons	trouvez	trouvent
to visit	visiter	visite	visites	visite	visitons	visitez	visitent

* The "*e*" is normally removed in the "*nous*" form, but it's kept here so the "*g*" remains soft.

Verbs

This page is about irregular verbs and using the infinitive and the imperative.

Irregular verbs

Here are some common **irregular** verbs in the present tense:

English	Infinitive	*je / j'*	*tu*	*il / elle / on*	*nous*	*vous*	*ils / elles*
to go	aller	vais	vas	va	allons	allez	vont
to have	avoir	ai	as	a	avons	avez	ont
to be	être	suis	es	est	sommes	êtes	sont
to do	faire	fais	fais	fait	faisons	faites	font
to put	mettre	mets	mets	met	mettons	mettez	mettent
to be able to	pouvoir	peux	peux	peut	pouvons	pouvez	peuvent
to know	savoir	sais	sais	sait	savons	savez	savent
to want	vouloir	veux	veux	veut	voulons	voulez	veulent

Infinitive

The **infinitive** form is just the 'to...' form of the verb. In the present tense, use it like you would in English:

> The infinitive can be used to give instructions too, e.g. in recipes.

> J'aime jouer au foot. (I like to play football.)

> *"Jouer"* ("to play") is in the infinitive form.

> The infinitive is also used in the future tense (see p.51).

Imperative

- The **imperative** is used to tell somebody to do something — it's used with the *"tu"*, *"nous"* and *"vous"* forms of the verb.
- Most imperative forms are similar to the **present tense**, but without *"tu"*, *"nous"* or *"vous"* before the verb. (See p.46 for more on pronouns.)

> tu écoutes (you listen) → Écoute! (Listen!)

> nous écoutons (we listen) → Écoutons! (Let's listen!)

> vous écoutez (you listen) → Écoutez! (Listen!)

> When the *"tu"* form of the verb ends in *"es"* you drop the *"s"*.

The Past

The perfect past tense is used to describe something that's already happened.

Formation

- There are **two parts** to the perfect past tense — the present tense form of "*avoir*" (or "*être*", see below) and the **past participle** of the main verb.

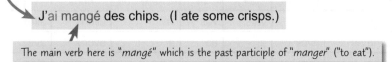

J'ai mangé des chips. (I ate some crisps.)

The main verb here is "*mangé*" which is the past participle of "*manger*" ("to eat").

- Using the present tense version of "*avoir*" is like saying that something "**has** been done". So "*j'ai mangé des chips*" is like saying "I **have eaten** some crisps". "*J'ai mangé*" can be translated as "I **ate**" or "I **have eaten**", depending on the **context** of the sentence.

Past participle

- French verbs can be divided into three groups depending on their **endings** — "*er*" verbs, e.g. "*manger*" ("to eat"), "*ir*" verbs, e.g. "*finir*" ("to finish") and "*re*" verbs, e.g. "*vendre*" ("to sell").

- For the past participle of regular "*er*" verbs, remove the "*er*" and add "*é*".

manger ⟶ mangé   jouer ⟶ joué

- For the past participle of regular "*ir*" verbs, remove the "*ir*" and add "*i*".

finir ⟶ fini

- For regular "*re*" verbs, remove the "*re*" and add a "*u*".

vendre ⟶ vendu

Être

- Some verbs use "***être***" ("to be") instead of "***avoir***" ("to have") to form the perfect past tense. All **reflexive** verbs (see p.47) use "*être*".
- With *être*, the past participle has to agree with the subject:

Add an 'e' for feminine subjects, and an 's' for plural subjects.

Je me lève. (I get up.) ⟶ Je me suis levé. (I got up.) (m)

Je me lève. (I get up.) ⟶ Je me suis levée. (I got up.) (f)

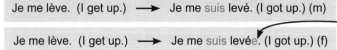

The Future

In some of the units, pupils will need to use the near future tense.
This page explains how it is formed.

The near future

- When the "**future**" tense is mentioned in the Scheme of Work, it's referring to the "**near future**" tense.

- The near future in English is when you say that you're "**going to**" do something.

- The near future tense is formed using the appropriate present tense version of "*aller*" ("to go") (see p.49), and the **infinitive** form of the main verb (see p.49).

Je vais jouer dans la cour. (I am going to play in the playground.)

"vais" is the first person present tense version of *"aller"*

The simple future

- The simple future tense is used to talk about that something that "**will** happen".

- Pupils **won't** have to use the simple future tense at this stage, but it does appear in the story lesson in Unit R — Family (Years 5-6).

"Tu iras au bal." ("You will go to the ball.")

This is the only place the simple future comes up in the program, so you don't need to worry about the formation of this tense.

Forming Questions

There are a few different ways to ask a yes/no question in French.

Intonation

You can ask a question by making your **voice rise** at the end of a sentence. This is the **easiest** way to ask a question — the words don't change.

C'est bon. (It's good.) ⟶ C'est bon? (Is it good?)

A statement instantly becomes a question if you make it sound like a question. We use this form a lot in *Salut!*

Inversion

You can **swap** the subject **pronoun** (see p.46) and the **verb** to form a question.

Tu as mal. (You are in pain.) ⟶ As-tu mal? (Are you in pain?)

This is just the same as you do in English.

Using "Est-ce que...?"

"*Est-ce que*" can be added to the beginning of a phrase to turn it into a question.

C'est la Chine. (It's China.)

↓

Est-ce que c'est la Chine? (Is it China?)

Literally, "est-ce que...?" means "is it that...?".
You can use it to turn any statement into a yes/no question.

Forming Questions

If you're looking for more than a "yes" or "no", you need to use a **question word**.

"Qu'est-ce que...?"

Add "***Qu'est-ce que***" to the beginning of a phrase to make it a "**what**" question:

tu aimes (you like)

↓

Qu'est-ce que tu aimes? (What do you like?)

> If you're asking someone to choose something, you don't use "*qu'est-ce que*", you use "*quel*" — see p.54.

"Qui?"

If you want to ask "**who?**" use "*qui?*".

C'est qui? (Who is it?)

"Quand?"

If you want to ask "**when?**" use "*quand?*".

C'est quand, ton anniversaire? (When is your birthday?)

"Pourquoi?"

"*Pourquoi?*" is used to ask "**why?**".

> You reply to a "*pourquoi*" question with "*parce que*" ("because").

Pourquoi tu aimes l'été?   (Why do you like summer?)

"Où'?"

Use "*où?*" if you want to ask "**where?**".

Où est la gare? (Where is the train station?)

> Don't forget to add the accent to the "*ù*" — "*ou*" (without an accent) means "or".

Forming Questions

"Combien?"

"*Combien?*" means "how much?" or "how many?".

> Ça coûte combien? (How much does it cost?)

"Comment?"

"*Comment*" means "**how**".

> Comment vas-tu à l'école? (How do you go to school?)

"*vas*" is the second person singular of "*aller*" ("to go") — see the verb table on p.49.

It's also used with "*être*" ("to be"), to ask **what something is like**.

> Ton chat est comment? (What is your cat like?)

"Quel? / Quelle?"

- "*Quel?*" means "**which?**" or "**what?**" — it's used when there's a **choice** between nouns.

- "*Quel*" is the **masculine singular** version of the word — it changes depending on the **gender** and **number** of the noun:

Masculine singular	Feminine singular	Masculine plural	Feminine plural
quel	quelle	quels	quelles

> C'est quel pays? (What country is it?)
>
> Quelle est ta matière préférée? (What is your favourite subject?)
>
> Quels bonbons préfères-tu? (Which sweets do you prefer?)
>
> Tu aimes quelles chaussures? (Which shoes do you like?)

Apostrophes

Apostrophes are used in more or less the same way as they are in English.

Apostrophes

- Apostrophes replace **missing letters**.

- In French, you sometimes need to use an apostrophe when a word **ending in a vowel** is followed by a word **beginning with a vowel**.

- You remove the **vowel** at the end of the first word and **replace** it with an **apostrophe**.

- This is why the **articles** for nouns beginning with a vowel look different (see p.37) — they're shortened versions of "*le*" or "*la*".

le (the) + animal (animal) ——→ l'animal (the animal)

- As well as "*le*" and "*la*", the most **common** words that follow this rule are: "*je*", "*ne*", "*de*", "*te*", "*me*", "*que*" and "*si*".

J'aime faire du skate. (I like skateboarding.)

Je n'ai pas d'animaux. (I don't have any animals.)

Je t'appelle Maurice. (I'll call you Maurice.)

Je m'appelle Aurélie. (My name is Aurélie.)

Qu'est-ce que c'est? (What is it?)

s'il vous plaît (please)

The "*e*" in "*ce*" is sometimes replaced with an apostrophe too — "*c'est*" ("it is"). But when it's used in front of a masculine singular noun that begins with a vowel it becomes "*cet*" — "*cet oiseau*" ("this bird").

- When "*h*" appears at the start of a word, it's usually treated as if it's **not there** (it's a "silent h"). This means the vowel following the "*h*" is treated as the first letter.

l'hôtel (the hotel)   l'hôpital (the hospital)

This is why words beginning with a silent h need "*l'*" as the article.

- There are a few **exceptions** though:

le hockey (hockey)   le hamster (the hamster)

Possession and Negatives

Possession

There's **no possessive apostrophe** in French
— "*de*" is used to show possession.

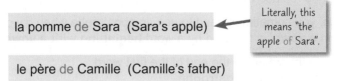

la pomme de Sara (Sara's apple) ← Literally, this means "the apple of Sara".

le père de Camille (Camille's father)

Negative sentences

To make a positive sentence into a negative one, you need
to **sandwich** "*ne*" and "*pas*" around the verb.

je mange (I'm eating) ⟶ je ne mange pas (I'm not eating)

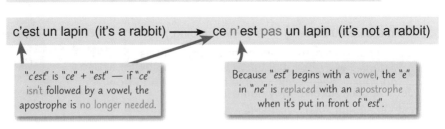

c'est un lapin (it's a rabbit) ⟶ ce n'est pas un lapin (it's not a rabbit)

"*c'est*" is "*ce*" + "*est*" — if "*ce*" isn't followed by a vowel, the apostrophe is no longer needed.

Because "*est*" begins with a vowel, the "*e*" in "*ne*" is replaced with an apostrophe when it's put in front of "*est*".

ne...plus

You might also see "*ne*" used with "*plus*" in
the same way. This means "**no longer**".

Le bateau ne fonctionne plus. (The boat no longer works.)

ne...personne

If "*ne*" and "*personne*" are used together in a
sentence, it means "**nobody**" or "**not anyone**".

La pantoufle ne va à personne. (The slipper doesn't fit anyone.)

Formal Language

Sometimes it's best to use slightly more formal language — teach pupils to use different language when they want to be polite.

"Tu" or "vous"?

- In French, there are **two** ways to say "you".

- If you're talking to **one** person in an **informal** situation, use "*tu*".

- If you're talking to **more than one person**, or to **one person** you **don't know**, you should use "*vous*". This is what you'd use with **shopkeepers** or **waiters** because it's more **polite**.

- The vocabulary in the **Classroom Language** Unit uses the "*vous*" form of the verbs — they're phrases that are useful for talking to your **whole class** at once (see next page).

Greetings

- Saying "*salut*" ("hi") is quite **informal**. Pupils can use it to greet each other, but teach them that it's better to use "*bonjour*" ("hello") with people that they **don't know**.

- In the same way, "*au revoir*" ("goodbye") is more **formal** than "*à bientôt*" ("see you soon").

- To be more **formal** when asking somebody how they are, say "*Comment allez-vous?*" rather than "*Ça va?*".

Present conditional

- Just like in English, you can use the conditional tense when you want to be **more polite**.

- "*Je voudrais*" is in the **conditional** tense and means "I would like". It's more polite than saying "*je veux*" ("I want").

Classroom Language

You might find the words and phrases from the **Classroom Language** Unit helpful if you want to speak to your pupils in French.

Instructions

- You can use the **vocabulary** in 'Lesson 1 — In the Classroom' to give instructions to your class.

- The instructions are in the **imperative** form, see p.49.

- Some of the instructions include a **pronoun** after the imperative form of the verb, e.g. "*levez-vous*" ("stand up"). This is because it's a **reflexive** verb, see p.47.

Talking to one child

- When you're talking to **more than one child**, use "*vous*" — the **plural** form of "you".

- But as an adult talking to one child, you **don't** need to use the **formal** "*vous*" (see previous page).

- So you should use "*tu*" if you're only talking to **one child**.

- Here are some **examples** of how the words and phrases from the Classroom Language Unit should change when you're only talking to one child:

English	To whole class	To one child
please	s'il vous plaît	s'il te plaît
listen	écoutez	écoute
look	regardez	regarde
stand up	lèvez-vous	lève-toi
show me	montrez-moi	montre-moi

Accents and Pronunciation

The easiest way to get a handle on French **pronunciation** is to hear lots of French words spoken by native French speakers.

Use the Phonics Unit on the disc for help with pronunciation

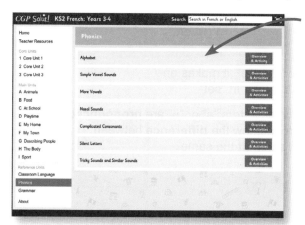

We've split the Phonics Unit into manageable chunks of similar sounds. You can listen to each sound in **isolation** as many times as you like, then hear it in the context of some full words.

> See page 30 for more about the Phonics Unit, and how you might use it with your class.

Over the next few pages, there's a brief guide to the **accents** that are used in French. Accents are important for spelling as well as pronunciation. You'll find audio examples in the **Phonics Unit**.

é

- An **acute accent** (´) is sometimes found on an "e" — "é".

- It changes the way the "e" is **pronounced** — "é" makes an "**ay**" sound.

> l'épaule (the shoulder)
>
> écouter (to listen)
>
> vous désirez (you want)
>
> un café (a coffee)
>
> un éléphant (an elephant)

Accents and Pronunciation

à, è, ù

- A **grave accent** (`) can be found on "*a*", "*e*" or "*u*".

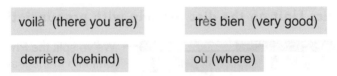

> voilà (there you are)   très bien (very good)

> derrière (behind)   où (where)

- When it's used on the letter "e", it makes an **open** "**e**" sound — like the "e" in "set".

- It **doesn't** change how the letters "a" or "u" are **pronounced** — it's sometimes there to show the **difference** between words that are otherwise **spelt** the same.

> où (where) ——→ ou (or)

> à (at) ——→ a ("has" — il / elle form of "to have")

â, ê, î, ô, û

- A **circumflex** (^) is sometimes placed on a vowel.

- It **doesn't usually** affect pronunciation, but it **is** important for the spelling of the word. An "**ê**" is pronounced in the same way as "**è**".

> un bâton de colle (a glue stick)
>
> la tête (the head)
>
> une boîte (a box)   Encourage pupils to include accents where necessary — words aren't spelt correctly without them.
>
> un fantôme (a ghost)
>
> août (August)

61

Accents and Pronunciation

ç

- A **cedilla** (,) is sometimes added to the letter "*c*" — "*ç*".

- It creates a **soft "*c*"** sound — like the "s" sound in English.

> le français (French)
>
> Ça coûte combien? (How much does it cost?)
>
> le garçon (the boy)
>
> la leçon (the lesson)

- A cedilla is **not** used when the "*c*" is **in front** of an "*e*" or an "*i*" because it already makes a soft "*c*" sound here — "*ce soir*" ("tonight").

œ

- When the letters "*o*" and "*e*" are next to each other, they're usually combined to make "**œ**".

> un œuf (an egg)

> ma sœur (my sister)

ë, ï, ü

- A dieresis (¨) sometimes appears on the letters "e", "i" and "u".

- It shows that a vowel is in a separate syllable to the vowel next to it — so **both** vowels must be **pronounced**.

> Noël (Christmas)

What Not to Pronounce

There are quite a few 'silent' letters in French that you need to be careful of.

"th"

In French, "*th*" is pronounced in the same way that "*t*" is pronounced in English — listen to the pronunciation of "*le théâtre*" ("the theatre").

Silent "h"

- The letter "*h*" is **not pronounced** when it comes at the start of a word.

- For example, "*l'heure*" ("the time") or "*huit*" ("eight").

> This is why "*l'*" usually replaces "*le*" or "*la*" with words that begin with "*h*" — see p.55 for more.

"ent" endings

- Most verbs end in "*ent*" when they're in the third person plural form of the present tense. For example, "*ils aiment*" ("they like").

- However, you **shouldn't** pronounce the "*ent*".

Words ending in "t" or "s"

- **Don't** pronounce "*t*" or "*s*" if they come at the end of a word.

- For example, "***violet***" ("purple") or "*le **bras***" ("the arm").

- There's **no difference** in the pronunciation of most words once they've been made plural — "***chien***" ("dog") and "***chiens***" ("dogs") sound the same.

> Loan words from English don't follow this rule. So the final letter of "*le tennis*" ("tennis") and "*le tee-shirt*" ("T-shirt") is pronounced.